THE ROYAL NAVY AT ROSYTH
1900 - 2000
by Martin Rogers

The second **HMS Ark Royal** moored downstream of the Forth Bridge in 1939. She was a new addition to the Royal Navy having been commissioned in November 1938. In the early days of the Second World War she served in the Home Fleet, the South Atlantic and the Mediterranean and with Force H. On 13 November 1941 she was torpedoed by **U-81** in the western Mediterranean and sank the following day while under tow.

(Douglas Cornhill Collection)

Author's Notes

When I was first asked to compile this book of photographs, I declined. Although I had a good knowledge of the history of Rosyth and the early days of the Dockyard, I was aware that my lack of detailed knowledge of the ships of the Royal Navy would be apparent to readers of this book. I eventually agreed to compile this book in the knowledge that I would be able to call on the expertise of others to check that the captions were accurate and informative. My thanks to Mike Critchley and Steve Bush of Maritime Books and Ben Warlow who have all helped in this way.

Much of the material for this book has been drawn from the photographic archives of the Dunfermline Carnegie Library and I am indebted to them for permission to reproduce photographs from their general archive and from the Douglas Cornhill and Morris Allan collections. Douglas Cornhill was a photographer based at **HMS Caledonia** in the late 1930s and Morris Allan is a well known professional photographer (now retired) in Dunfermline. The two collections are largely held in negative format and my special thanks go to Chris Neale at the Library for all his assistance in arranging for copies of the photographs to be produced for me.

I am also grateful to the following bodies and individuals who have lent photographs and/or given permission for them to be reproduced in this book:

Babcock Rosyth Ltd (Babcock)
Fleet Air Arm Museum (FAAM)
Imperial War Museum (IWM)
Inverkeithing Local History Society (ILHS)
Ministry of Defence (MoD)
Keith Hall
William Hutchinson
Eric Simpson
Dr G Watson

My thanks also go to Babcock's photographer Mike Tazioli who took most, if not all, of the photographs contributed by Babcock.

Martin Rogers
Rosyth
2003

The Royal Navy at Rosyth 1900 - 2000

For centuries, ships have used the Firth of Forth as a waterway and natural anchorage. In the middle of the 2nd Century AD, the Forth marked the northern boundary of the Roman occupied territory and would have been used to bring supplies to the Roman settlements and garrisons on the south side of the Forth. Princess Margaret (later Queen Margaret of Scotland) first set foot on Scottish soil in about 1069 when the ship bringing her and her family from England anchored in a bay to the west of North Queensferry. In the 13th and 14th Centuries the Forth was used by English forces in their efforts to subjugate Scotland as did Oliver Cromwell's forces in 1651 when they landed in Fife. There they fought and defeated a Scottish Royalist army in what became known as the Battle of Inverkeithing or Pitreavie.

The Royal Navy recognised the advantages of the Firth of Forth and at the beginning of the 20th Century used it as an anchorage during exercises etc. There was a more permanent presence in the form of a Forth Guardship (*HMS Anson* and later *HMS Sappho*) and the wooden second rate ship of the line (*HMS Impregnable*) which was re-named *HMS Caledonia* and served as a boys' training ship between 1891 and 1906. She was moored on the south side of the Forth near the harbour of Port Edgar. At that time the naval dockyards were situated on the south coast - a long way away from the North Sea which was the most likely area of conflict with the German fleet. The Government decided to build a new Dockyard on the east coast and various locations were considered including the Humber, Forth and Cromarty. In March 1903, an announcement was made that the new naval port and base was to be built at St Margaret's Hope on the north side of the Forth. There was opposition to this, not least from Lord Fisher, the First Sea Lord. Critics argued that if the Forth Bridge was attacked and collapsed, it could prevent ships of the Fleet leaving the Forth and the Dockyard. Some preliminary work was undertaken in the following years but it was not until 1909 that the main works began. The principal contract was awarded to Messrs Easton Gibb and Sons of Newport and they started work in March of that year with the works due for completion in March 1916. When the Great War began in August 1914 the Dockyard was still under construction but the tidal basin intended for submarines was able to be brought into use. Shortly afterwards the repair ship *HMS Aquarius* was berthed alongside one of the jetties.

At the outbreak of war, the Grand Fleet was based at Scapa Flow but in 1915 the Battlecruiser Fleet under Vice Admiral Sir David Beatty was transferred to the Forth to be nearer at hand to deal with German raids on the east coast of England. The formal opening ceremony of the Dockyard was performed by King George V on 8 June 1915 and the Dockyard finally became operational in March 1916 when the main basin was flooded. The depot ship *HMS Crescent* was the first to enter the main basin and shortly afterwards *HMS Zealandia* was the first to dock in No 1 dock following a mishap in the Forth. These were the first of many ships to enter the Dockyard including (less than 3 months later) ships from the Battlecruiser Fleet which had sustained damage during the Battle of Jutland. The Dockyard was not the only facility to be provided. A Wireless Telegraph Station was erected on Castlandhill Rosyth, a Royal Naval Ordnance Depot was built at Crombie and a Torpedo Boat Destroyer Base (*HMS Columbine*) was constructed at Port Edgar with a Naval Hospital nearby at Butlaw. An experimental hydroplane (seaplane) station operated from Port Laing near North Queensferry (later transferring to the Dockyard) and, also at North Queensferry, there was a Kite Balloon Station. A Royal Naval Air Station was established at Donibristle at the end of 1917 becoming part of the newly formed Royal Air Force in April 1918.

On 21 November 1918 the Forth was the setting for the formal surrender of the German Fleet before it was interned at Scapa Flow. The Dockyard provided valuable service to ships of the Royal Navy during the war (and in the post war period). However, in 1925 the Dockyard and the Torpedo Boat Destroyer Base at Port Edgar were placed on a care and maintenance basis and the Royal Navy presence virtually disappeared. In 1928, thirty-five S, T and V class destroyers were based at Rosyth in reserve but during the care and maintenance period, the main activity in the Dockyard was shipbreaking. It is ironic that the facilities of a Dockyard established to repair and refit Royal Naval ships should have been used by Metal Industries to scrap them. In 1937 the liner *Majestic* was brought to Rosyth to act as a temporary home for the boy sailors and artificer apprentices of a new shore establishment to be named *HMS Caledonia*. The threat of war prompted the re-opening of the Dockyard on a limited basis in 1938 and it became fully operational in 1939.

Once again the Dockyard proved a valuable asset in the war effort. About 3000 Royal Naval and other vessels were repaired or refitted at Rosyth during the Second World War. The Admiralty Under Water Works were opened at the South Arm site in 1943 to examine the characteristics of shock and forces to which submarines and warships were subjected (especially from under water explosions). In 1946 it changed its name to the more familiar title of the Naval Construction Research Establishment (NCRE). Towards the end of the war there were fears that the Dockyard might again be closed. Fortunately, this did not happen and during the 1950s a considerable number of new buildings were constructed in the Dockyard to replace temporary wartime buildings. New married quarters were also provided in the Hilton Road area in the 1950s and 60s. In 1963, Rosyth was chosen as the lead Yard for refitting and refuelling nuclear submarines and a massive expansion and modernisation programme followed. The name *HMS Cochrane* had been used for depot/accommodation ships in Rosyth but in 1968 the name was given to a new shore establishment built just outside the Dockyard. At around the same time the Boom Defence Depot, *HMS Safeguard*, paid off and its remaining naval functions were transferred to *HMS Cochrane*. There was further investment in buildings and facilities in the 1970s. *HMS Lochinvar* at Port Edgar was closed in 1975 and a new Fleet Base was established in the Dockyard to support the Mine Countermeasure and Fishery Protection Squadrons previously based at Port Edgar. Around this time the Cod War started in Icelandic waters and new classes of ships (Castle and Island) were built primarily for fishery protection and oil rig duties. The Dockyard played a significant part in preparing ships for the South Atlantic Task Force during the Falklands War in 1982. In 1984, *HMS Caledonia* closed and the site became part of *HMS Cochrane*. In 1986, plans were announced for further expansion and modernisation of the Dockyard in connection with its intended role in refitting Trident submarines.

The 1990s saw a marked change in the fortunes of the Dockyard and Naval Base. Reductions in the size of the Royal Navy meant a reduction in refitting work. Work was well under way on new docking facilities for the Trident submarines to the west of the Dockyard (Project RD 57) when, in 1993, the Government decided to transfer this work to Devonport. (A recent National Audit Office report highlighted a massive increase in costs of providing facilities at Devonport which calls into question the wisdom of this decision). To compensate for the loss of the Trident submarines refitting, Rosyth was guaranteed a programme of surface ship work until 2007. The Naval Base closed in 1995 and the last Royal Navy vessels to be based at Rosyth sailed out of the Forth in November of that year. In 1996 H*MS Cochrane* was closed and a Royal Naval Support Establishment (*HMS Caledonia*) was commissioned on the site of the former *HMS Caledonia*. Among the naval work carried out at Rosyth Dockyard in the final years of the century, has been the refitting and repairs of the Swiftsure Class of submarines and the refitting of the aircraft carrier *HMS Ark Royal*. Sadly it has also become the resting place of Resolution and Valiant Class submarines following their de-commissioning. The submarine graveyard along the south side of the basin is a poignant reminder of the days when the refitting of the submarines formed the major workload for the Dockyard. However, 100 years after the announcement that a new Dockyard was to be built at Rosyth we can end on an optimistic note. It is expected that the Dockyard will be involved in assembling the new super aircraft carriers planned for the Royal Navy and thus will continue to play a significant role in supporting the Royal Navy in the years to come.

A postcard view of the Forth at the beginning of the 20th Century. The Forth Road Bridge now spans the Forth at this point and the property in the centre of the photograph (known as "The Hope") no longer exists. The top of the cantilevers of the Forth Bridge can be seen to the left of the photograph and the boys' training ship *HMS Caledonia* on the right. The *Caledonia* was formerly the second rate ship *HMS Impregnable* and was stationed in the Forth from 1891 to 1906.

(Dunfermline Carnegie Library)

An artist's impression of the new Rosyth Naval Base c 1908. The layout of the Dockyard may appear to be inaccurate but it is based on the plans released by the Admiralty in 1908. It was only when construction commenced that some changes were made such as the re-positioning of the direct entrance from the south to the east side of the basin and the cutting off of the south west corner of the basin. The 15th Century Rosyth Castle can be seen in the left centre of the picture.

(Author's Collection)

This photograph of sailors disembarking at Hawes Pier, South Queensferry for a run ashore c1912 appeared in a Special Naval Edition of the Sphere magazine in 1913.

A 70 hp Short biplane fitted with floats at a beach at Port Laing near North Queensferry where a temporary base was set in 1912. The aeroplane was involved in exercises to see if a submarine could be detected from the air. This photograph appeared in the Sphere magazine of 1913 where the plane was described as a hydro aeroplane.

This postcard view was taken from the Forth Bridge in about 1913 and as well as ships of the Royal Navy, shows the coastguard station at North Queensferry which was later taken over as an Admiralty Signal Station.

(Author's Collection)

In July 1914, the 7th Submarine flotilla moved from Dundee to their war station at Rosyth. Here we see submarine *C28* en route to Rosyth. One of 20 submarines of the Second Group of the C class, this particular Vickers-built vessel survived the war, being scrapped in 1921.

(IWM Neg Q115080)

There are a number of photographs of ceremonies in No 3 Dock but unfortunately the nature of the ceremonies are not disclosed. This photograph was taken on 15 July 1915 (a Thursday) so it could not have been for a Sunday service. No 3 Dock was the last of the docks to be completed and at the time of this photograph, work on it was still in hand.

(Dunfermline Carnegie Library)

The basin at Rosyth was flooded in September 1915 and on 17 March 1916 the cruiser **HMS Crescent** which served as the Dockyard Depot Ship was the first ship to enter it (through the direct entrance). *Crescent* was to remain as Depot Ship at Rosyth until 1920 when she was sold to a German shipbreaking firm. She was replaced by the battleship **HMS Glory** which was re-named **HMS Crescent**.

(Dunfermline Carnegie Library)

Some technical difficulties with the construction of the entrance lock delayed its completion. On 27 March 1916, after a mishap in the Forth, the King Edward VII Class battleship *HMS Zealandia* became the first ship to pass through the lock and be docked at Rosyth (in No 1 Dock). When she was launched in 1904, she was named *HMS New Zealand* but her name was changed in 1911 to allow the name to be given to another ship under construction.

(Dunfermline Carnegie Library)

HMS Warspite, a super dreadnought battleship of the Queen Elizabeth Class, was badly damaged during the Battle of Jutland and entered dry dock for repairs on returning to Rosyth in June 1916. This view down her starboard side shows two of her 6-inch guns with the Dockyard workshops in the background.   (Dunfermline Carnegie Library)

HMS Warspite was one of the few battleships to be spared the axe after the Great War and served with the Atlantic and Home Fleets. She was extensively modernised in the 1930s and served throughout the Second World War. At Narvik in April 1940 she accounted for 8 German destroyers and in March 1941 took part in the Battle of Matapan at which units of the Italian Fleet were destroyed. She was bombed twice but was in action during the D-Day landings at Normandy where she was damaged by a mine. She went into reserve in 1945 and was sold for scrap in 1946. (Dunfermline Carnegie Library)

The battlecruiser **HMS Lion** was the flagship of Vice Admiral Sir David Beatty and is seen here at Rosyth in July 1916 after the Battle of Jutland. During the battle the roof of Q turret (pictured) was pierced by a shell from the German battlecruiser, *Lutzow*, which killed or wounded all but two of the officers and men manning the gun. Although fatally wounded, Major F J W Harvey, of the Royal Marine Light Infantry gave orders to flood the magazine thus avoiding an explosion which would have destroyed the ship. For this action he was awarded the Victoria Cross.

(Dunfermline Carnegie Library)

The Chatham Class light cruiser **HMS Southampton** served with distinction in the Battles of Heligoland Bight, Dogger Bank and Jutland. During a night action in the Battle of Jutland she sustained serious casualties from around 40 shell hits. Although the structure of the ship stood up quite well to 5.9-inch shell fire and no guns were damaged, the open back style of gun shield provided little protection to the upperdeck gun crews of whom many were killed or injured. The ship is seen here in Rosyth Dockyard awaiting repairs. She was sold for scrapping in 1926.

(Dunfermline Carnegie Library)

The battlecruiser **HMS Princess Royal**, although damaged, escaped the fate of two other battlecruisers **HM Ships Queen Mary** and **Indefatigable** which were sunk during the Battle of Jutland. Note the nets and poles along her deck which when swung outwards acted as a defence against torpedoes when at anchor. The **Princess Royal** was to spend her last days at Rosyth where she was broken up in 1923 (see page 32).

(Dunfermline Carnegie Library)

COOK 1769

TASMAN 1642

1840

NEW ZEALAND

The Battlecruiser *HMS New Zealand* was paid for by the country of New Zealand and it was intended that she should be based in their waters. After she was completed in February 1912 she undertook a 10 month cruise of the dominions but was then attached to the First Battlecruiser Squadron and later to the Grand Fleet. She saw action at the Battles of Dogger Bank and Jutland. She was listed for disposal under the Washington Treaty and was sold for breaking up at the end of 1923. In this photograph of the quarter deck we see the ship's crest with the motto "Onward".

(Dunfermline Carnegie Library)

The date of this photograph is uncertain but it was probably taken on 16 June 1916 when King George V visited part of the Grand Fleet at Rosyth following the Battle of Jutland. His escort is probably Admiral Sir Robert Lowry, Commander-in-Chief Coast of Scotland. The King is abut to be introduced to Dockyard officials and local dignitaries.

(Dunfermline Carnegie Library)

The British and Foreign Sailors' Society opened this Sailors' Rest at Charlestown in January 1917 - the first of its kind in Scotland. It had a large hall accommodating some 400 men together with a room for the use of the petty officers, games, a library and a canteen serving food and non-alcoholic beverages. It was provided as a base ashore for sailors of a light cruiser squadron moored in the western part of the Forth.

A Kite Balloon Station at North Queensferry in May 1917. This was one of 11 such stations under Admiralty command between 1914 and 1920. The role of RNAS kite balloons included U-boat spotting and convoy protection, for which role they were flown from monitors. A total of twenty vessels were equipped with balloon winches at the time, including nine battleships. The inset shows the group of officers manning the station.

(Dunfermline Carnegie Library)

The Active Class Cruiser *HMS Fearless* in dock in Rosyth after a collision near May Island in the Forth in January 1918. A large scale night exercise was under way involving units of the Grand Fleet and the Battlecruiser Fleet based at Rosyth. The unexpected appearance of a number of minesweeping trawlers crossing their path caused chaos among the ships of the Battlecruiser Fleet. A number of collisions took place with two K Class submarines of the 12th and 13th Submarines Flotillas being sunk and three damaged, the tragic encounter subsequently becoming known as "The Battle of May Island". *HMS Fearless* leading the 12th Flotilla collided with and sank the submarine K17. (IWM Neg Q56608)

An aerial view from an airship of part of the Grand Fleet in the Forth in about 1918. Rosyth Dockyard can be seen in the distance. Normally the smaller ships were moored upstream of the Forth Bridge and the capital ships downstream opposite Inverkeithing, Dalgety Bay and Aberdour.

(IWM Neg 19563)

Three Royal Naval battlecruisers manoeuvring into position for the formal surrender of the German Fleet in the Forth on 21 November 1918. On the way 14 squadrons of the Grand Fleet were formed up in 2 columns and went out to meet the German Fleet west of May Island. The German Fleet then had to pass between the 2 columns to their anchorage off Inchkeith. Who would have guessed that some twenty years later many of the German ships would pass this way again but floating upside down having been salvaged at Scapa Flow and brought to Rosyth to be broken up.

(IWM Neg Q20620)

An aerial view from an airship of the newly constructed torpedo destroyer base at Port Edgar, commissioned in December 1917 as **HMS Columbine**. A total of 66 destroyers could be berthed at one time and the combined number of personnel ashore and afloat was 6000. During the Second World War it was commissioned as **HMS Lochinvar** and was used for minesweeping training. In October 1943, *Lochinvar* moved temporarily to Granton and the base was taken over as a training base (known as **HMS Hopetoun**) for the D-Day landings on Sword Beach. Many of the buildings are still in use today as part of the Port Edgar Sailing Centre.

(IWM Neg: Q19554)

The battleship **HMS Canada** at Rosyth in 1919. **HMS Canada** was originally built for Chile as the **Almirante Latorre** but with the outbreak of war, she was purchased by the British government in September 1914. She took part in the Battle of Jutland, firing 42 rounds of 14-inch and 109 rounds of 6-inch shell, without being hit herself. After a refit in 1919/20 she was returned to Chile. She was sold to a Japanese scrap dealer in 1959, the last surviving Dreadnought to have served with the Battle Fleet at Jutland. (Dunfermline Carnegie Library)

The aircraft carrier **HMS Argus** was built in Glasgow and was intended to be an Italian passenger liner, *Conte Rosso*. Her construction was halted with the outbreak of the Great War but in 1916, she was purchased unlaunched and converted into an aircraft carrier - the first in the world to have a full length flight deck on which aircraft could land and take off with relative safety. She was commissioned in September 1918 shortly before the Armistice and this photograph of her at Rosyth was probably taken in 1919 or 1920. After a period of about 10 years in active service she was laid up for a time before being used as a training carrier. She was brought back into front line service in 1942 when she served with Force H and supported the landings in Africa. She was put into reserve in 1943 and sold for scrapping in 1946.

(FAAM)

HMS Hood passing through the entrance lock at Rosyth in January 1920. She was fresh from the builders yard and was about to be docked to have her bottom coated before undergoing sea trials. In anticipation of her docking, work had been carried out the previous year to cut a notch in the end of No 2 dock to accommodate her.　　　　　　(Dunfermline Carnegie Library)

The battlecruiser **HMS New Zealand** and the battleships **HMS Neptune** and **Hercules** in the basin at Rosyth in about 1920. **Neptune** and **Hercules** were in the Reserve Fleet at this time and both were scrapped in 1922. **New Zealand** was listed for disposal under the Washington Treaty and was sold for breaking up in 1923. (Author's Collection)

HMS Courageous was one of 3 light cruisers designed to be part of a shallow draught armada to land an army on the Baltic coast of Germany during the Great War. The plan was dropped after Admiral Lord Fisher left the Admiralty but the ships were completed. *Courageous* is seen here in dock at Rosyth (probably in 1921) before she was converted to an aircraft carrier between 1924 and 1928. She was to be the Royal Navy's first major casualty of the Second World War being sunk by *U-29* to the west of Ireland on 17 September 1939, only 2 weeks after war was declared.

(Author's Collection)

HMS Princess Royal, ***HMS Agincourt*** and ***HMS New Zealand*** being broken up at Rosyth in about 1923. There was a substantial rundown in the activities of the Dockyard in 1922 and parts of the basin (and later the docks) were leased to shipbreaking firms. Rosyth Shipbreaking Company bought the battlecruisers ***New Zealand***, ***Princess Royal*** and ***Agincourt*** in 1923. The Company had leased the inside of the south wall of the basin for their activities and this photograph shows the three ships at various stages of demolition. (Keith Hall)

HMS Colossus, the lead ship of that class of battleship, arriving at Rosyth in September 1928 to be broken up. First commissioned in 1911, she fought at the Battle of Jutland and in 1921 following a period in reserve at Devonport was placed on the disposal list. However, by September she had been reprieved to serve as a Boys Training Ship at Portland. In 1922 she again found herself at Devonport on the disposal list. A second reprieve in 1923 saw her employed as a hulk attached to the Training Establishment ***Impregnable***. By 1927 her days were numbered and in 1928 she was purchased by the Alloa Shipbreaking Company and broken up over a period of 12 months. (Morris Allan)

During 1927, thirty five S, T and V Class destroyers were held in reserve at Rosyth. They were periodically docked in a floating dock and the tug *Buckie Burn* (seen here) was transferred from Sheerness in 1928 to assist with this. A number of the reserve destroyers can be seen in the background.
(Author's Collection)

After the German fleet surrendered in November 1918, they were interned at Scapa Flow. In June 1919 the German Admiral Von Reuter gave orders for the German fleet to be scuttled. Salvaging them was no easy matter but in 1927 the first battleship was raised and towed to Rosyth to be broken up. This was the first of many ships to be brought to Rosyth. The identity of this ship is not certain but is probably the battleship *Friedrich der Grosse* which arrived at Rosyth in August 1937. The reserve destroyers can be seen on the east and south sides of the basin.

(Douglas Cornhill Collection)

The Government decided to establish a training facility in Scotland for boy entry seamen and artificer apprentices. As a temporary measure whilst shore facilities were being built, the liner *Majestic* (formerly the German liner *Bismarck*) was commissioned as **HMS Caledonia** in April 1937. The ship could accommodate over 2500 officers, crew, boy seamen and apprentices. The photograph shows Divisions on the parade ground probably in 1937.

(Douglas Cornhill Collection)

Some of the officers of *HMS Caledonia* in 1937. The only one who can be named is the Chaplain of the boys training establishment, Rev JNC Holland (second from the left in the back row). The Captain is probably Sir Atwell H Lake. (IWM Neg: HU75152)

A brass band was started in the early days of **HMS Caledonia** and continued throughout the life of the establishment. It began with the formation of a drum corps and here we see the corps (and one piper) leading the parade, probably in 1938. The band were asked to play at many local and national events including Dunfermline Civic Week, the Royal Tournament and the Horse of the Year Show.

(Douglas Cornhill Collection)

A field gun competition was a feature of life at **HMS Caledonia** and this photograph shows the boys in action on the parade ground in the Dockyard probably in 1938. When she was commissioned in 1937, **HMS Caledonia** had the dual role of training boy seaman and artificer apprentices. On the outbreak of war, the training of the boy seamen was transferred to the Isle of Man but the training of the apprentices continued at Rosyth. (Douglas Cornhill Collection)

Although the Royal Navy was making only limited use of Rosyth Dockyard during the 1930s, the Forth was still used as an anchorage. The Home Fleet anchored here in October 1938 en route from the completion of exercises in the Moray Firth area. Here we see **HMS Royal Oak,** a Royal Sovereign Class battleship, at anchor in the Forth. She was an early casualty of the Second World War being torpedoed by **U-47** in Scapa Flow in October 1939 with the loss of 833 officers and men.   (Douglas Cornhill Collection)

The battleship **HMS Rodney** was commissioned into the Royal Navy in 1937 and is seen here in the Forth in 1938. **Rodney** saw action with the Home Fleet and Force H during the Second World War including the operation to sink the **Bismarck** in May 1941. She was put into reserve after the war and was to return to the waters of the Forth in 1948 to be scrapped at Inverkeithing.

(Douglas Cornhill Collection)

The Kent Class cruiser **HMS Cornwall** was completed in 1928 and underwent a major modernisation in the mid 1930s, a few years before this photograph was taken at Rosyth in 1938. Note the guest warp boom slung out from the ship's side to provide access to the ship's boats. *Cornwall* served in the East Indies, South Atlantic and Eastern Fleet in the early years of the Second World War. She was sunk in April 1942 to the west of Ceylon after an attack by Japanese bombers.

(Douglas Cornhill Collection)

The aircraft carrier **HMS Furious** in the Forth in 1938. **HMS Furious** was built as a large light cruiser but in 1917 took on a pioneering role in naval aviation. In February 1917 her forward gun was removed and replaced with a flying off deck. On 2 August of that year Squadron Commander Dunning made history by landing on **Furious** - the first aircraft landing on a ship. Sadly he was killed a few days later when attempting to repeat the feat. **HMS Furious** was modified after the accident by the addition of a landing on deck on the stern. A full flight deck was fitted in the early 1920s. She had a variety of roles in the Second World War, including hunting U-boats in the Atlantic, carrying gold bullion to Canada, carrying out air strikes against German shipping in Norway (including the **Tirpitz**) and ferrying replacement aircraft to Malta during Operation Pedestal in August 1942. She was scrapped at Dalmuir in 1948.

(Douglas Cornhill Collection)

The newly built F Class destroyer **HMS Foresight** at Rosyth probably in 1939. The three white bands on the after funnel identify the flotilla to which the ship was attached, in this instance the 8th Destroyer Flotilla. This photograph and those on succeeding pages are not dated but would seem to have been taken on the occasion of a visit to the Forth by the Home Fleet in August 1939 during their autumn cruise. This was only a matter of days before the start of the Second World War. The Fleet was due to move on to Invergordon, Scapa Flow and exercises in the North Sea. **HMS Foresight** was one of a number of new destroyers being commissioned in the late 1930s. She foundered on tow after being torpedoed by Italian aircraft during Operation Pedestal in August 1942.

(Douglas Cornhill Collection)

The cruiser **HMS Edinburgh** was another new addition to the Fleet. She was to play a major part in many actions during the early years of the Second World War seeing service in the Atlantic and Arctic and with the Malta Convoys. While on convoy duty to Murmansk in April 1942 she was torpedoed by the U-boat **U-456** and later sank with the loss of 57 lives and her cargo of £5 million in gold bullion.

(Douglas Cornhill Collection)

A large number of trawlers were pressed into service as minesweepers etc. Trawler *T-16* seen in the Forth in 1939 would seem to be in need of a boiler clean.   (Douglas Cornhill Collection)

The Depot Ships **HMS Ambrose** (left) and **HMS Greenwich** at Rosyth in 1939. *Greenwich* had been the Depot Ship at Rosyth since 1927 and was joined by **Ambrose** in 1928 following the closure of the base at Port Edgar. **Ambrose** was later re-named **HMS Cochrane**. Shortly after this photograph was taken *Greenwich* moved to Scapa Flow.

(Douglas Cornhill Collection)

The Thames Class submarine *HMS Severn* at Rosyth in 1939. She operated with the Home, Mediterranean and Eastern Fleets during the Second World War sinking 3 ships and an Italian submarine in 1940 and 1941. At the end of 1943 she was involved in running supplies to the Aegean islands. Her active service ended in April 1945 and she was scrapped in Bombay in 1946.
(Douglas Cornhill Collection)

The submarine depot ship **HMS Forth** at Rosyth in 1939 with 2 submarines, *Seahorse* (98S) and *Starfish* (19S), alongside. She was first commissioned in 1939 serving as the depot ship for the 2nd Submarine Flotilla and transferring in 1941 to the 3rd Submarine Flotilla. For a time she was based at Halifax Nova Scotia where she supported submarines being used to protect convoys against surface raiders. After the war she went to the Mediterranean and was involved in the Suez operations. She spent several years in the Far East and returned to Devonport in 1971 being used as a Fleet Maintenance Base and being re-named **Defiance**. She was broken up in the Medway in 1985. (Douglas Cornhill Collection)

49

HMS Guardian, seen here at Rosyth in 1939, was the first ship to be built specifically for laying anti-submarine nets around naval vessels in unprotected anchorages. Built at Chatham she was commissioned in 1933 for special trials amd service with the Home Fleet Target Service. During the Decond World War she saw service in the East Indies, the Mediterranean for Operation Husky (the landings at Sicily) and with the British Pacific Fleet. In 1947 she was reduced to reserve at Devonport, being scrapped at Troon in December 1962.

(Douglas Cornhill Collection)

The Battleship **HMS King George V** in dock at Rosyth in October 1940 to complete her fitting out. She then served in the Home Fleet taking part in the pursuit of the **Bismarck** in May 1941 and operating on the Murmansk convoys. She was part of Force H in 1943/44 before moving to the Pacific theatre. She went into the Reserve Fleet in 1946 and was scrapped in 1958 at Dalmuir. Note the prominent degaussing cable - **King George V** being the only one of the class to have it fitted outside of the hull. The dazzle pattern camouflage scheme was painted over in overall grey before the end of 1940. (IWM Neg: A1494)

The Prime Minister Winston Churchill visited Rosyth on 23 October 1940 and inspected this unnamed warship (possibly *HMS King George V* which was in dock at the time - see previous photograph). He is followed by Vice Admiral Sir Charles Gordon Ramsey.

(IWM Neg: HU4980)

On a visit to Rosyth on 5 March 1941, His Majesty King George VI inspected the crew of the battlecruiser **HMS Hood**, the pride of the Royal Navy. The earlier photo of **Hood** on page 29 was taken at the very beginning of her naval service. This one was taken near the end as, less than 3 months later (on 24 May 1941), **Hood** was sunk by the **Bismarck**. Most if not all of these men would have been killed as there were only 3 survivors.

(IWM Neg: A3370)

Warships Weeks were held in various parts of Fife in 1941 to raise money for the war effort. Here a Royal Navy contingent makes its way down Inverkeithing High Street during the Inverkeithing, North Queensferry and Hillend Warship Week in November 1941. Dunfermline Burgh (which included Rosyth) adopted the destroyer **HMS Malcolm** and Inverkeithing Burgh, the armed trawler **HMS Elm**.

(IWM Neg: A6417)

A lighter moment during the days of the Second World War was the unveiling of a sculpture of Barnacle Bill and Popeye outside the Fleet Cinema in March 1942. The two figures were chosen to symbolise the links between the Royal Navy and the US Navy. The sculpture was the work of Alexander Proudfoot assisted by Tom Purvis. (William Hutchinson)

HMS Lochinvar at Port Edgar was a training base for the Royal Navy's minesweeping crews. In this photograph taken in 1942, officers are being instructed on the features of various types of mines.

(IWM Neg: A9310)

The battleship **HMS Anson** (King George V Class) in the Forth in June 1942, shortly after completion. She spent most of her time on the Murmansk Convoys later being transferred to the British Pacific Fleet. She remained in the Far East until 1946 returning to Portsmouth on 29 July. She was allocated to the Training Squadron, later becoming the Flagship. In November 1949 she was relieved by **Vanguard** and paid off into reserve, eventually being handed over for scrapping in December 1957. (Author's Collection)

The RAF station at Donibristle was taken over by the Royal Navy in May 1939 and was commissioned as *HMS Merlin*. In this unusual photograph a group of Wrens employed as radio mechanics and operators are seen returning from flying duties in June 1942. Margaret Parkinson (second from the left) is carrying a parachute in one hand and a Very pistol in the other. The plane behind the Wrens is a Swordfish and the nose of a Walrus can be seen on the right. (IWM Neg: A10817)

The battleship **HMS** *Duke of York* of the King George V Class leaving dock at Rosyth in November 1943. The armament visible includes 5 Oerlikons, 4 x 14-inch guns and an 8 barrel pom pom mounting on Y turret. **HMS** *Berwick* is in the dock in the background. The *Duke of York* was commissioned in November 1941 and, like her sister ship **HMS** *Anson*, she served most of the Second World War in the Home Fleet taking part in the Murmansk Convoys and the operation leading to the sinking of the *Scharnhorst* in December 1943 (shortly after this photograph was taken). After a period in the Pacific she was the flagship of the Commander in Chief Home Fleet in Chief Home Fleet in the late 1940s. She was then placed in reserve and scrapped in 1958 at Faslane.

(IWM Neg: A20163)

A view from the 100 ton crane of the battleship *HMS Nelson* moored on the west wall of the basin in May 1944. She was completed in 1927 and was the flagship of either the Atlantic or Home Fleets for 14 years alternating with *HMS Rodney.* She had an eventful war being mined twice (in 1939 and 1944) and in June 1944 she participated in the bombardment before the invasion of France. On VJ day she went to Penang where the surrender of Japanese forces in South East Asia was signed aboard her. After a brief spell as flagship of the Home Fleet she joined the training squadron. Later she was used as a bombing target before being scrapped in 1949. Like her sister ship *Rodney* she ended her days in the shipbreaker's yard in Inverkeithing.

The Illustrious Class aircraft carrier ***HMS Indomitable*** in the basin at Rosyth in May 1944 about to enter No 2 dock. She is carrying Avenger aircraft on her flight deck. She served in many theatres during the War including the Eastern Fleet, the Malta Convoys, the Mediterranean and the Pacific Fleet winning 5 battle honours. She was reduced to reserve in 1953 and sold for scrapping at Faslane in 1955.

(IWM Neg: A23377)

An aerial view of **HMS Merlin**, the Royal Naval Air Station at Donibristle, in May 1944. During the Second World War the airfield provided a temporary home for a number of Fleet Air Arm Squadrons prior to embarkation on aircraft carriers. It was also the permanent home of 782 Communications Squadron and the Royal Aircraft Repair Yard. In 1944 some 2000 civilian staff and 1000 service men and women worked in the Repair Yard. During the course of the war they repaired, inspected or reconditioned more than 7000 aircraft of almost all types and variants in the Fleet Air Arm. There is an unusual runway layout with both runways being oriented east/west at only a shallow angle to each other. This was because of the constraints of the surrounding terrain with rising ground to the north.

(FAAM)

Ferry pilots of **HMS Merlin**, the Royal Naval Air Station at Donibristle pose before a Seafire aircraft in 1944. At the back is Lt George Hunt. In the front (from the left) is Sub Lt G D Spence, Sub Lt F Morris, Lt Duncan, 2nd Officer Walton (Air Transport Auxiliary), Sub Lt J Stevenson and Lt J Hughes. (Dunfermline Carnegie Library)

63

With the end of the Second World War there is some return to normality with Rosyth holding its first ever Navy Days in 1948. These took place over 3 weekends between May and August and a total of some 27000 people attended. This is a diving display, presumably by divers from **HMS Safeguard**.

(Dunfermline Carnegie Library)

Pitreavie Castle was bought by the Air Ministry in 1938 and became the headquarters of 18 Group Coastal Command. An underground bunker was completed in 1941 housing the Maritime Headquarters with Royal Air Force and Royal Navy staff working in close cooperation. The hunt for the *Bismarck* and raids against shipping in occupied Norway were planned here and the Battle of the Atlantic was largely mounted from here. With the formation of NATO in 1948, Pitreavie became the headquarters of the North Atlantic Area. In this photograph (date unknown) the bands of the RAF Regiment and Royal Marines are presumably performing a Beating the Retreat Ceremony. (ILHS)

The Royal Yacht *Britannia* at Rosyth in June 1955, the year after she was first commissioned. Her Majesty Queen Elizabeth and Prince Philip are greeted at Rosyth by Vice Admiral W G A Robson, Flag Officer Scotland, and Lord Elgin, Lord Lieutenant of Fife. After carrying out a number of official engagements in Scotland, the Queen and Prince Philip set off in the Royal Yacht on a State Visit to Norway. The *Britannia* decommissioned in December 1997 and is now open to the public in Edinburgh's port of Leith, only a few miles away from Rosyth.

(Morris Allan Collection)

During the Second World War, new buildings were erected on a site overlooking the Royal Naval Artificer Training Establishment as it was known. In 1946 it was again given the name **HMS Caledonia** and, in 1955 the original figurehead of **HMS Ganges**. However, it was found to be too decayed and not capable of restoration. The apprentices helped to make this replica which stood at the main gate of *Caledonia* for a number of years. This photograph was taken at the unveiling ceremony.

(Morris Allan Collection)

HMS Maidstone, the flagship of the Commander in Chief Home Fleet, leaving Rosyth in May 1957. The Home Fleet had assembled in the Forth for their summer cruise and exercise programme. *Maidstone* had a long and varied career with the Royal Navy. During the Second World War she was stationed at Rosyth, Gibraltar, Algiers, Trincomalee, Freemantle, Philippines and Hong Kong. After a spell as flagship of the Home Fleet she was reconstructed and based at Faslane. Following a period in reserve she was used as an Army accommodation ship and then as a prison ship at Belfast. Her long career came to an end when she was broken up at Inverkeithing in 1978. (Morris Allan Collection)

Also in the Forth in May 1957 for the Home Fleet assembly was the Colossus Class aircraft carrier *HMS Ocean*. She was commissioned in August 1945 and in December of that year became the first carrier to receive landings from jet aircraft. Another "first" came in 1952 when on a tour of duty off Korea. A propeller driven Sea Fury fighter from *HMS Ocean* shot down a MiG-15 fighter, the only time a piston engined aircraft had shot down a jet engined aircraft. She acted as a commando carrier during the Suez crisis in 1956 and after a period in reserve was broken up at Faslane in 1962.

(Morris Allan Collection)

The Hunt Group frigate **HMS Talybon**t replaced **HMS Easton** as the training ship for the apprentices of **HMS Caledonia**. She is seen here in the basin at Rosyth in October 1957. She ended her days at the breakers' yard at Charlestown in 1961. The ship outboard of her has been mothballed.   (Morris Allan Collection)

The Battle Class destroyer *HMS Armada* in the Forth in May 1958. The Home Fleet had assembled for a Spring weapon training cruise. *Armada* entered service in July 1945 fitted out as a destroyer leader. She was placed on the reserve list in 1960 and sold for breaking up in 1965.

(Morris Allan Collection)

Also in the Forth in May 1958 for the gathering of the Home Fleet is the Fiji Class cruiser *HMS Kenya*. She was the flagship of the Flag Officer Flotillas Home Fleet. She was involved in the Russian convoys and Operation Pedestal, the convoy to Malta, during the Second World War and took part in a raid on Vaagso in Norway. She was decommissioned in 1959.

(Morris Allan Collection)

The Commanding Officer of the Weapons Class destroyer **HMS Battleaxe**, Commander J E Maldwell, reads the warrant at the commissioning of the ship at Rosyth in March 1959. During a 2 year refit at Rosyth she had been modernised as a radar picket ship. She was first commissioned in 1947 and served in British, European and Mediterranean waters for 9 years. She was broken up in 1964 having been seriously damaged in a collision with the frigate *Ursa* two years earlier.

(Morris Allan Collection)

An extensive programme of building married quarters at Rosyth took place in the 1950s and 60s. Among the houses built were these houses in Forbes Road in 1959. Hilton Road runs across the foreground of the photograph.
(Dunfermline Carnegie Library)

The Earl and Countess Mountbatten of Burma visiting Rosyth in April 1959. They arrived at Turnhouse Airport and crossed the Forth from Port Edgar in the minesweeper *HMS Chailey.*
This was the Earl Mountbatten's last official engagement as First Sea Lord during which he visited *HMS Cochrane* at Donibristle and the Naval Construction Research Establishment at
St Leonard's in Dunfermline and officially opened the new Electrical Workshop in the Dockyard.

(Morris Allan Collection)

The commissioning of **HMS Tudor** in January 1960 was held below decks because of high winds. The external photograph proves the point with the Union Flag standing out stiffly. **HMS Duncan** is in the background. The Press report of the occasion refers to separate services being held for Protestant and Roman Catholic members of the crew........

(Morris Allan Collection)

..........This interior photograph would appear to be of the Roman Catholic service held in the "periscope room" by Rev Father Daly of Aberdour. **HMS Tudor** was about to join the 5th Submarine Squadron at Portland. She was scrapped at Faslane in 1963.
(Morris Allan Collection)

The name **HMS Cochrane** is synonymous with Rosyth but for a time (1954-1962) it was based at the former Royal Naval Air Station at Donibristle. This photograph of the quarterdeck of **Cochrane** taken in 1961 dates from that period in **Cochrane's** history.

(Author's Collection)

The French submarine *Saphir* being handed back to the Royal Navy in August 1961. A number of Royal Naval submarines were loaned to the French Navy in the early 1950s including *HMS Satyr* which was renamed *Saphir* by the French Navy. She was formally handed back at this ceremony in Rosyth Dockyard. She had been launched in September 1942 and during war service sank *U-987* west of Narvik in June 1944. She was broken up at Charlestown (about 2 miles along the coast) in 1962.

(Morris Allan Collection)

The time honoured tradition of stirring the Christmas pudding is performed by Captain RHP Elvin, Commanding Officer of *HMS Caledonia* in November 1961. This was to be served to the 560 officers and men of the shore establishment. The ingredients included 3 pints of rum, 12 bottles of stout and 80 silver threepences.

(Morris Allan Collection)

After an 18 month refit the Blackwood Class Frigate **HMS Dundas** is recommissioned at Rosyth in January 1962. The recommissioning service was held indoors in the Fleet Canteen building because of strong winds. **Dundas** was due to leave for Portsmouth where she was to be used to train officers and men in anti-submarine warfare. (Morris Allan Collection)

The Cruiser **HMS Tiger** arrives at Rosyth in September 1963. She was launched in 1945 but work on her was stopped in 1946. In 1954 it was decided that she should be completed and she was first commissioned in 1959. She saw service in the Far East in the early 1960s. In December 1966 she was at the centre of the world's stage when she was used as a conference centre at Gibraltar for talks about Rhodesia between Prime Minister Harold Wilson and Mr Ian Smith. She was converted to a Command Helicopter Cruiser in 1968-72 and was put into reserve in 1978.

(Morris Allan Collection)

The first nuclear powered submarine in the Royal Navy, **HMS Dreadnought**, arrives at Rosyth in December 1963, six months after she was completed. This was for a routine docking for cleaning and re-coating the hull and examination of underwater fittings. She was decommissioned in 1983 and it is ironic that 40 years after her first visit she again lies at Rosyth with some of her successors until a decision is reached about the fate of the redundant nuclear submarines.

(Morris Allan Collection)

HMS Palliser was in No.2 Dock at Rosyth for a maintenance period between 26 February to 10 July 1964. In 1958/59 the small, single screw Type 14 frigates had their hulls strengthened to stand up to the severe weather encountered whilst conducting Fisheries Protection duties off Iceland. Of her original armament her torpedo tubes had been landed and the 3rd 40mm Bofors mounted on the quarterdeck was removed after cracking developed in the stern section of some of the class. The destroyer **HMS Caprice** can be seen ahead of **Palliser**. (Dr G. Watson)

A Royal Marine band performs at the commissioning ceremony of the Whitby Class frigate **HMS Eastbourne** in 1964. She had undergone a refit at Rosyth to equip and modify her as a ship of the Dartmouth Training Squadron. She was sold for scrap in 1985 and ended her days at the breakers' yard at Inverkeithing. (Morris Allan Collection)

The Boom Defence Vessel **HMS Barnstone** in the basin at Rosyth in June 1965. She was a coal fired ship and one of the oldest ships in commission. In the 1960s she was used as a training ship for technical ratings under instruction at the Boom Defence Depot **HMS Safeguard**. In the background under the watchful eye of the Dockyard's 250 ton crane are **HMS Delight**, **HMS Mohawk** and **HMS Gurkha**.

(Author's Collection)

The lead ship in her class, the frigate **HMS Blackwood**, commissioning at Rosyth in September 1965. She was to succeed **HMS Duncan** as leader of the Fishery Protection Squadron based at Port Edgar.

(Morris Allan Collection)

The modified Battle Class destroyer **HMS Corunna** at Rosyth for refit in August 1965. She was first commissioned in 1947 and in 1960 was modernised at Rosyth to be a Fleet Radar Picket with new radar (including a double bedstead) and a Seacat anti aircraft missile mounting aft. She was laid up in Portsmouth in 1969 and scrapped at Sunderland in 1984.

(Morris Allan Collection)

HMS Londonderry and the tug ***Accord*** seen in the basin at Rosyth in June 1967.She returned to Portsmouth to enter a two year refit and modernisation period, emerging in 1969 with a flightdeck and hangar. From November 1975 - October 1979 she was again at Rosyth where she was refitted for service as a Trials Ship for the Admiralty Surface Weapons Establishment. She recommissioned at Portsmouth on 11 October 1979. The superstructure aft of the funnel had been removed and replaced by a long deckhouse supporting two large pylon masts for her role as a Radar Training and Trials ship.

(D. Swetnam)

In May 1967, the frigate **HMS Rapid** (formerly an R Class destroyer) commissioned as a day runner for **HMS Caledonia** to assist in certificating the apprentices. She had been completed in 1943 and employed in convoy duties with the Eastern Fleet in the later years of the Second World War. She was converted to an anti-submarine frigate in 1951 but was then placed in reserve in 1953. Following an exercise in 1970, she had a race with the Chatham based destroyer **HMS Cavalier** for the title of "The Fastest Ship in the Fleet". This was held in the Firth of Forth on 6 July 1971 in perfect weather. Over a period of 2 hours and a distance of 64 miles the ships were neck and neck but unfortunately **Rapid** lifted a safety valve and **Cavalier** won the race by a mere 30 yards. The average speed of the race was 31.8 knots. **Rapid** celebrated her 30th and last birthday at Rosyth in 1973. (Morris Allan Collection)

The former Type 15 frigate **HMS Roebuck** undergoing shock trials in 1968. The opening of the Admiralty Undex Works (AUW) in 1943 at Rosyth, marked the beginning of half a century of research into underwater explosion effects. AUW was established at the South Arm site of the dockyard leased by the shipbreaking company Metal Industries. The site offered a substantial sea wall for underwater explosion trials and 40 ft of water at high tide. In 1946 the scope of the work was extended to cover the wider field of naval structures under the new title of Naval Construction and Research Establishment (NCRE).

(MoD/Crown Copyright)

The Tribal Class frigate **HMS Zulu** commissioned at Rosyth in June 1970 after a refit and was to join the Western Fleet in the NATO area. Meantime the routine of the ship continues with pay parade for the crew. **HMS Zulu** was completed in 1964 and was placed in reserve in 1979. She was sold to the Indonesian Navy in 1985 and served as the **Martha Kristina Tiyahahu**. How did they fit all of that on the cap tally? (Morris Allan Collection)

Underwater explosive trials in 1971 on the decommissioned destroyer **HMS Scorpion** at the Oxcars trials site off Aberdour. This series of tests was one of many undertaken by the NCRE to examine the ship's resistance to underwater explosions. The work on the effects of explosions on ships' hulls has involved many ships over the years, from the cruiser **Orion** in 1949, through the destroyers **Oudenarde** and **ex-Jutland** in the 1950s, **Obdurate**, **Roebuck** and **Broadsword** in the 1960's and **Scorpion**, **Defender** and the frigate **Blackpool** in the 1970s. The former Leander class frigate **HMS Naiad** was converted and renamed **Hulvul** for a series of explosive trials in 1989.   (IWM Neg: MH30032)

Her Majesty Queen Elizabeth the Queen Mother at the re-commissioning of *HMS Resolution* in 1971. The Queen Mother had launched the submarine at Barrow -in -Furness in September 1966 and attended the re-commissioning of the submarine in July 1971 after its first refit. Here she inspects Rosyth Dockyard through the submarine's periscope. *Resolution* was the first of the Royal Navy's Polaris submarines and the first to be refitted at Rosyth. This marked the beginning of a number of successful refits of such submarines at Rosyth.

(MoD/Crown Copyright)

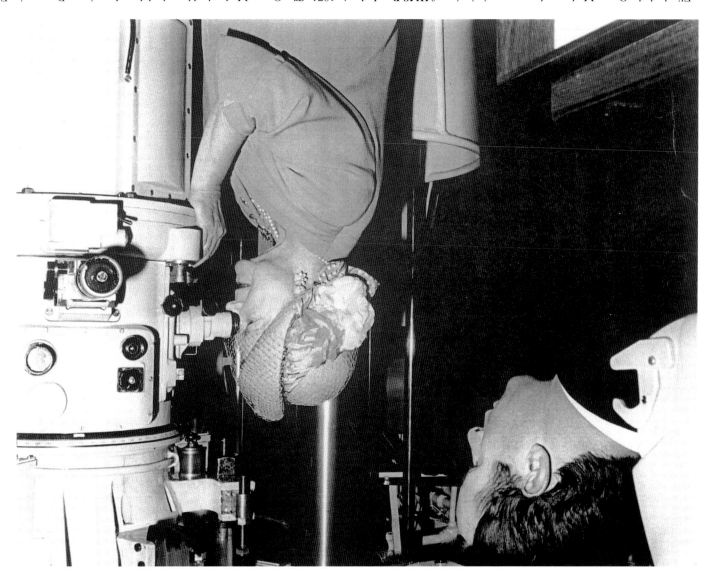

An unusual occurrence at Rosyth in March 1973 when two warships with the same name met up - the Porpoise Class submarine *HMS Narwhal* and the nuclear powered attack submarine *USS Narwhal*. It was not only the name they had in common. In both cases the submarines were the third to bear the name and both belonged to their respective 2nd Submarine Squadrons. The commanding officer of *HMS Narwhal*, Lt Cdr Thomas LeMarchand, shakes hands with his opposite number Commander Edward Kellogg. In his other hand he holds a tusk from the almost extinct Arctic narwhal whale. *HMS Narwhal* was completed in 1959 and had an unusual ending being sunk 15 miles south of Falmouth in 1983 and used for the training of salvage personnel.   (Morris Allan Collection)

HMS Lochinvar, the naval base at Port Edgar as seen from the Forth Road Bridge in July 1974. She was home to the Fishery Protection and Mine Countermeasures Squadrons until the base closed at the end of 1975. The squadrons moved to the new Fleet Base in Rosyth Dockyard. (Author's Collection)

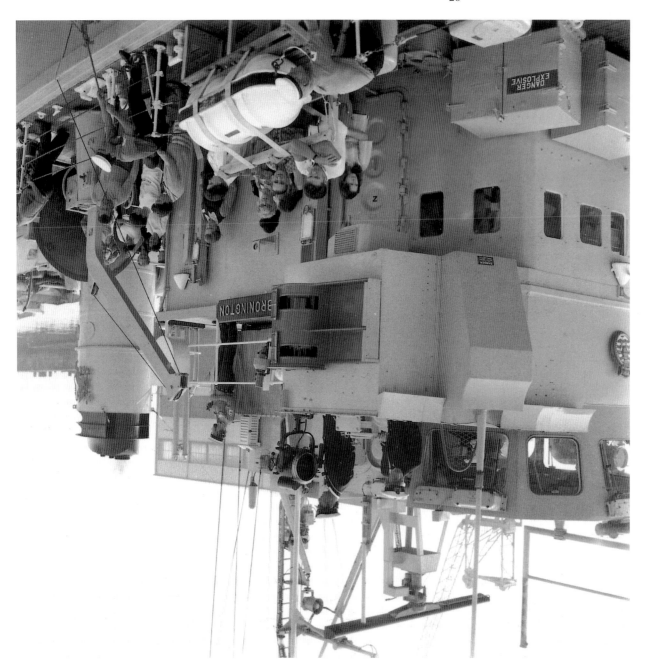

For a brief spell the Coniston Class Mine Countermeasures Ship *HMS Bronington*, became one of the best known ships in the Royal Navy when His Royal Highness Prince Charles took command of her in July 1976. Prince Charles is seen here on the bridge as the ship returns from a families cruise on the Forth. *HMS Bronington* was completed in 1964 and re-named *HMS Humber* being assigned to RNVR Humber Division of the 101st Minesweeping Squadron. She reverted to her original name in 1958 and saw service around the coasts of Britain, north western Europe and Scandinavia. In 1966 she joined the First Mine Countermeasures Squadron at Port Edgar which re-located to Rosyth in 1975. No doubt because of her Royal connection she was purchased by The Bronington Trust and is now moored at Birkenhead. (Morris Allan Collection)

The Leander Class frigate **HMS Diomede** off North Queensferry in April 1976. This was at the time of the Cod Wars and she had been rammed 4 times by the Icelandic gunboat **Baldur** whilst protecting British trawlers. The rubbing strake on **Baldur's** stern had caused a gash 20 feet long and 3 feet high in **Diomede's** side as can be seen from the photograph. The wardroom suffered the most damage. The portrait of the Queen was intact but that of Prince Philip was stated to have been lost in action. (Morris Allan Collection)

66

HMS Odin, an Oberon Class submarine lies in the basin at Rosyth in July 1978 while in the final stages of refit. In the background are *HMS Caledonia's* harbour training ships *HMS Eastbourne* and *HMS Duncan* (see following page).

(Author's Collection)

Over a period of years a number of ships at the end of their working lives served as training ships for **HMS Caledonia.** Here we see the Type 12 frigate **HMS Eastbourne** and the Type 14 frigate **HMS Duncan** in the basin at Rosyth in July 1978. *Eastbourne* took over from **HMS Rapid** as the afloat training ship but in 1977 her hull was found unfit for sea service and she became an additional harbour training ship. She had been completed in 1958 and was sold for breaking up in 1986. *Duncan* arrived at Rosyth in 1971 to act as the harbour training ship. She had been completed in 1958 and was broken up in 1985.

(Author's Collection)

Full House......**HMS *Lochinvar*** at Port Edgar was closed in 1975 and the Mine Countermeasure Vessels based there transferred to a new Fleet Base at Rosyth. Some of these ships are pictured here in the late 1970s or early 80s. The two Coniston or Ton Class ships nearest the camera are **HMS *Bildeston*** and **HMS *Shavington*. *Bildeston*** has the emblem of the Mines Countermeasures Squadron on her funnel whilst **Shavington** has the pennant of the Fishery Protection Squadron.   (Keith Hall)

HMS Thornham, one of the last of the "Ham" Class of inshore minesweepers, at Rosyth in 1980. At the time this photograph was taken this class of minesweeper was being used for training young seamen and RN University Unit personnel. The Fleet Base and Dockyard boathouse can be seen in the background. (MoD/Crown Copyright)

In October 1980, the Coniston Class MCMV **HMS Gavinton** made history at Rosyth by being the first ship to be refitted in Rosyth Dockyard's new syncrolift complex. The £12 million refit shop revolutionised working conditions. Small ship refits could now take pace under cover in the 5 berth garage rather than in the open or in floating dry-docks in the main basin. **Gavinton** was first commissioned in 1954 and served with the Training Squadron based at **HMS Vernon** before being placed in reserve in 1962. She was converted to a minehunter in 1968, and served in the Persian Gulf before coming to Rosyth in 1971.

(Morris Allan Collection)

The Dockyard's 100 ton crane is the viewpoint for this photograph of the Tribal Class frigate *HMS Gurkha* in the basin at Rosyth in the late 1970s. This aerial perspective affords a good view of the unusual deck layout of these frigates. The requirement to mount a 4.5-inch gun on the quarterdeck prevented the fitting of a conventional flight deck and hangar arrangement. To overcome this, the flightdeck was mounted above a small hangar, and the ship's Wasp helicopter descended into the hangar from above. Also of note are the Seacat surface-to-air missile system mounted just aft of the mainmast on each side and the Variable Depth Sonar mounted at the stern.

(MoD/Crown Copyright)

The Royal Navy's first hydrofoil *HMS Speedy* is seen at Rosyth in November 1980 during a 3 month trial period with the Fishery Protection Squadron. The experimental hydrofoil was commissioned by the Right Honourable Vere Cochrane, great, great grandson of Lord Cochrane who commanded the first *Speedy* in 1801. (Morris Allan Collection)

The minelayer **HMS Abdiel** in the Forth in 1981. She was a unique ship being designed as a Headquarters and Support Ship for mine countermeasure forces. She entered service in 1967 and had a major refit in 1978. She was sold out of the Royal Navy in 1988.

(MoD/Crown Copyright)

HMS Rothesay arrives at Rosyth in August 1981 after a 5 month deployment in the Gulf of Oman. **Rothesay** gave her name to the Type 12 Class of frigates laid down in the 1950s and named after coastal towns around Britain. During a limited refit at Chatham in the late 1970s her radar and communications were updated and a new 4.5-inch twin gun turret fitted. She was part of the 6th Frigate Squadron based at Rosyth, the other ships in the squadron being **HMS Plymouth** and **HMS Yarmouth** (both featured in later photographs).

(MoD/Crown Copyright)

The Rothesay Class frigate **HMS Plymouth** returns from the Falklands on 14 July 82 to a tumultuous welcome from a flotilla of small craft and a large crowd of people. She played an eventful role in the Falklands War firing the first shots in the battle to regain the Falklands and surviving 4 direct hits from bombs which fortunately did not explode. The Argentinian surrender of their forces in the Islands of St Georgia was signed on board her. **HMS Plymouth** is currently at Birkenhead having been acquired by the Warship Preservation Trust.

(Dunfermline Carnegie Library)

It is the turn of another Rothesay Class frigate, **HMS Yarmouth**, to receive a warm welcome on her return from the Falklands on 28 July 1982. In 1976 she had clashed (literally) with Icelandic gunboats during the Cod War. She was also in the thick of the action during the Falklands War and despite many close shaves remained unscathed. Her crew affectionately nicknamed her "The Crazy Y". She was first commissioned in 1960 and saw service in many parts of the world. Her final decommissioning came in 1986 and, ironically, she was sunk as a target in 1987.

(MoD/Crown Copyright)

In April 1982, the Dockyard had the task of converting five Humberside trawlers to serve as minesweepers in the Falklands. They were officially commissioned into the Royal Navy as the 11th Mine Countermeasures Squadron. Here we see (from right to left) *HM Ships Farnella, Junella, Northella, Pict and Cordella* returning to Rosyth in August 1982 after their time serving under the white ensign. As well as minesweeping they carried out other duties including transferring troops and stores from ship to shore. (MoD/Crown Copyright)

The Island Class patrol vessel **HMS Shetland** heading for Rosyth. In the background is the oil terminal at Hound Point. This class of ship was built on trawler lines to operate in the North Sea and protect the oil installations there. **Shetland** was completed in 1977.

(MoD/Crown Copyright)

The Tribal Class Frigate **HMS Gurkha** leaves Rosyth in September 1982. She was completed in 1963 and for many years was a Rosyth based ship. Her days seemed to have come to an end in July 1980 when she went to Chatham to join the standby squadron. After a period on the disposals list she was given a reprieve because of the losses experienced in the Falklands War. She was towed to Rosyth for a mini refit and once again heads for the open sea under her own steam. In 1985 she was sold to the Indonesian Navy and served as the **Wilhelmus Zakarias Yohannes**. (MoD/Crown Copyright)

Ships of the Fishery Protection Squadron arriving at Rosyth in March 1983. Five of the ships had been on exercise in the Antwerp area and they were joined by another three returning from fishery protection patrols for this grand entrance. The leading ship **HMS Dumbarton Castle** had already passed from the photographer's view and the Island Class patrol vessel **HMS Orkney** appears to be leading the column.

(Morris Allan Collection)

The Ton Class MCMV **HMS Lewiston** in the Forth in early 1980s. She was first commissioned in August 1960 taking her name from the village of Lewiston on Loch Ness.
(MoD/Crown Copyright)

Another Ton Class MCMV, *HMS Crichton*, made the headlines in 1983 when she adopted a mascot badges. *Crichton* started life in 1953 as *HMS Clyde* and *HMS St David* before becoming *Crichton* in 1977 on joining the Fishery Protection Squadron. Following an extensive refit at Rosyth in 1980 she joined the First Mine Countermeasures Squadron. At that time it was a tradition for ships of the squadron to have bridge badges and Robertsons Jam gave permission for *Crichton* to use the Robertsons Golly badge as its mascot emblem. A limited edition (only 50 produced) of an *HMS Crichton* badge with the golly wearing a sailor's uniform was produced for distribution to members of the ship's company. These badges have now become much sought after by collectors and are exchanging hands for sums in excess of £900! *Crichton* was broken up in 1987. (Morris Allan Collection)

The County Class destroyer **HMS _Fife_** passing North Queensferry in July 1983 on her way to take part in Rosyth Navy Days. She was first commissioned in 1966 and became one of the most travelled ships in the Royal Navy visiting virtually every corner of the world. She was refitted and modernised at Portsmouth in 1975/76 during which she was fitted with the Exocet surface to surface missile. At the time this photograph was taken she had just completed a 2 year mid life modernisation. After she was decommissioned in the early 1980s, she was sold to Chile.

HMS St David passes under the Forth Bridge as she leaves Rosyth.
She was a commercial trawler (formerly ***Suffolk Harvester***) on
charter to the Ministry of Defence and manned by the Royal Naval
Reserve. She was equipped for deep team sweeping and worked as
one of a pair with ***HMS Venturer*** (formerly ***Suffolk Monarch***).
(MoD/Crown Copyright)

"Are you sure you closed the hatch before we left?" *HMS Resolution* in the flooded dock at Rosyth in August 1984, conducts a check dive as she nears the end of her refit.
(MoD/Crown Copyright)

The Resolution Class submarine **HMS Repulse** arrives at Rosyth towards the end of 1984 to begin her third refit. She was the second of her class to come into commission and with her sister ships *Resolution, Renown* and *Revenge* provided Britain's nuclear deterrent for a period of some 28 years. She was the last of the Polaris submarines to be decommissioned (in August 1996) when the Resolution Class was replaced by the new Vanguard Class carrying Trident missiles. All four submarines are now laid up at Rosyth. (MoD/Crown Copyright)

A new class of fleet minesweepers, the River Class, joined the Royal Navy during 1985. They were steel built and based on commercial trawler design and were deployed with the Royal Naval Reserve. The exception was this ship, **HMS Blackwater**, which had a Royal Navy crew. She was commissioned in July 1985 and joined the 10th Mine Countermeasures Squadron based at Rosyth.

(MoD/Crown Copyright)

An unusual view of different sizes and styles of pick anchors in Rosyth Dockyard in July 1986. The 15th Century Rosyth Castle is in the background.   (Dunfermline Carnegie Library)

With the opening of the Syncrolift Complex in 1980 the era of the floating docks at Rosyth seemed to be over. The last floating dock at Rosyth (AFD 22) was towed away in July 1981. However, with an increase in the workload at Rosyth, floating dock AFD 26 was brought up from Portsmouth in 1984. Here we see an Oberon Class submarine entering or leaving the dock in 1987 assisted by tugs Alsatian and Georgina.

(Babcock)

HMS Churchill arrives at Rosyth in March 1989 to begin a £75m refit which was due to last 3 years. She is assisted by the harbour tug *Dexterous*. *Churchill* was a Valiant Class submarine developed from *HMS Dreadnought* and was capable of high underwater speeds and long endurance. In September 1990 the refit of *Churchill* was cancelled following cuts in the Defence Budget. She was de-commissioned at Rosyth at the end of 1991 and is laid up there.

(Babcock)

The Castle Class patrol vessel **HMS Dumbarton Castle** passes through the direct entrance lock (probably in 1991) with the assistance of the Dog Class tug **Alsatian**. The Castle Class comprises only 2 ships (the other being **Leeds Castle**) and was designed for fishery protection and offshore patrols within the UK territorial waters. The Dog Class was a general harbour tug.

(Babcock)

The entrance gate to **HMS Cochrane** in May 1993 with the gymnasium at the end of the access road and the Lion Club on the right. The tall building in the background with the multi-pitched roof is the main Naval Stores building. All of these buildings have now disappeared to make way for new developments. The buildings of **HMS Cochrane** have been demolished and the Innova Campus of Rosyth Europarc stands in its place housing call centres for the Bank of Scotland and Intelligent Finance.   (Author's Collection)

The Island Class patrol vessel *HMS Orkney* leaves the syncro-lift in 1995 looking like new.
(Babcock)

An unusual task for the Dockyard was a Ship Life Extension Programme of the landing ship *RFA Sir Bedivere*. As this photograph taken in 1995 clearly shows, the ship had to be cut in two and a 13 metre section was inserted to increase her length. The project had a number of unexpected difficulties including a large increase in the amount of steel work which had to be replaced. (Babcock)

Tuesday 7 November 1995 was a sad day for Rosyth when the Naval Base closed. The last ships to be based there were transferred to new bases - the 3rd Mine Countermeasures Squadron to Faslane and the 1st Mine Countermeasures Squadron and the Fishery Protection Squadron to Portsmouth. To mark the occasion a ceremonial sail past was held with the ships of the various squadrons sailing past **HMS Bicester** flying the flag of the Flag Officer, Scotland, Northern England and Northern Ireland Vice Admiral Chris Morgan. **HMS Middleton** is the ship in the fore in this photograph.

(Dunfermline Carnegie Library)

A poignant view of the sterns of ships leaving Rosyth on 7 November 1995. It seems almost as if the Royal Navy is turning its back on Rosyth Dockyard and the 80 years of service it had given as a Naval Base. Although ships are no longer based at Rosyth, the work of repairing and refitting them continues as can be seen from the remaining photographs in this book.

(Dunfermline Carnegie Library)

The Type 42 destroyer *HMS Edinburgh* leaves Rosyth at the end of 1995 or early 1996 on completion of a 54 week refit at Rosyth. She had been handed over by the builders Cammell Laird at Rosyth in 1985 and commissioned at Edinburgh's port of Leith a few months later. *Edinburgh* was one of a number of Type 42 destroyers to be based at Rosyth during the latter half of the 1980s and the early 1990s. (Babcock)

An aerial view of Rosyth Dockyard in 1997 taken from the north. The Fleet Base in the left centre of the photograph is deserted with the departure of the Mine Countermeasure and Fishery Protection Squadrons. The three graving docks in the centre are occupied by the seven redundant nuclear powered submarines with other naval vessels occupying other berths. On the south wall of the basin are the seven redundant nuclear powered submarines with other naval vessels occupying other berths. At the right centre of the photo is RD57 (the hole in the ground) - the aborted project to provide docking facilities for the Trident submarines. (Babcock).

The Swiftsure class submarine **HMS Sceptre** commenced a refit in No.2 Dock in June 1997 at the start of a three year refit. In March 2000 towards the end of the refit she broke her moorings while the main engine and prop shaft were being tested. In the dock with her is the World War Two vintage LST 3 class landing craft **Stalker** which was used as a support vessel during submarine refits.

(Author's Collection)

The **RFA Fort Victoria** passing through the entrance lock into the main basin in 1999. She is equipped to carry a wide range of armaments, fuel and spares offering a one stop replenishment for Royal Naval ships. This photograph gives a good view of the South Arm and the buildings of the Defence Evaluation and Research Agency (formerly NCRE). In the left foreground are a number of the former nuclear powered submarines laid up at Rosyth (see photograph on the following page). (Babcock)

The graveyard corner of the basin at Rosyth in the late 1990s where laid up nuclear submarines have ended their days. Nearest the camera are the former Polaris SSBNs *Revenge* and *HMS Resolution* and behind them are *Swiftsure*, *Dreadnought* and *Churchill*.

(Babcock)

The Invincible Class aircraft carrier **HMS Ark Royal** arrives at Rosyth in May 1999 for a two year refit. She is assisted by the tugs **Deerhound** and **Elkhound** amongst others. Her refit was part of the surface ship refit programme allocated to Rosyth following the transfer to Devonport of the Trident submarine refitting work. (Babcock)

Index